D1411340

Chicago Tribune

CAPONE

A PHOTOGRAPHIC PORTRAIT OF AMERICA'S MOST NOTORIOUS GANGSTER

MIDWAY

AN AGATE IMPRINT

CHICAGO

Printed in the United States of America

Chicago Tribune
Tony W. Hunter, Publisher
Gerould W. Kern, Editor
R. Bruce Dold, Editorial Page Editor
Bill Adee, Vice President/Digital
Jane Hirt, Managing Editor
Joycelyn Winnecke, Associate Editor
Peter Kendall, Deputy Managing Editor

Library of Congress Cataloging-in-Publication Data
Capone : a photographic portrait of America's most notorious gangster / edited by the Chicago Tribune Staff ; introduction by Jonathan Eig.
    pages cm
Includes bibliographical references.
Summary: "The story of gangster Al Capone told through photographs from the Chicago Tribune archives"-- Provided by publisher.
ISBN-13: 978-1-57284-146-8 (hardcover)
ISBN-10: 1-57284-146-X (hardcover)
ISBN-13: 978-1-57284-424-7 (ebook)
ISBN-10:1-57284-424-8 (ebook)
1. Capone, Al, 1899-1947--Pictorial works. 2. Gangsters--United States--Pictorial works. 3. Organized crime--United States--History--20th century--Pictorial works. I. Chicago Tribune (Firm)
HV6248.CI7C37 2013
364.1092--dc23
                                    2013020466

10 9 8 7 6 5 4 3 2 1

Midway is an imprint of Agate Publishing. Agate books are available in bulk at discount prices. For more information visit agatepublishing.com.

CONTENTS

ABOUT THIS BOOK

The images of Al Capone in this book were digitized from glass-plate negatives and original prints made from glass plates. These plates had been stored for decades in the deepest of basement storage rooms at the Tribune Tower, five levels below Michigan Avenue. Protected in paper envelopes, the plates were filed haphazardly. They were only recently located and brought up to the newsroom for scanning.

We had located buried treasure. Despite some degradation of the emulsion around the edges, most were in remarkably good shape. Because of the size of the plates and advances in digital scanning, incredible detail can now be seen—spats, hats and smirks.

We also scanned a small number of prints in folders filed in our old fourth-floor library. A few of those images had been published before, but only once, and then stored away in the stacks. The original glass plates associated with those prints have not been found, but the prints were so interesting and of such high quality that we included them in this collection.

In addition, during Capone's lifetime, photographic techniques evolved from glass plates to 4-by-5-inch black-and-white film negatives. By the time Capone died, in 1947, all of the photo coverage of his funeral was recorded on film.

The images were taken by photographers from the *Chicago Tribune* as well as the now-defunct *Chicago Herald-Examiner* and *Chicago American*. Those newspapers' archives were folded into *Tribune* archives when they went out of business.

Try to comprehend the difficulty of making glass-plate negatives in that era. News events were especially challenging—news photographers carried heavy Speed Graphic cameras that held 4-by-5-inch glass plates. Only one plate could be exposed at a time, so for every new photograph, another plate had to be loaded. It was commonplace for press photographers to shoot fewer than a dozen plates on assignment. Compare that with the hundreds of digital images typically made by today's *Chicago Tribune* photojournalists on their daily assignments.

Some of these digitized glass-plate images have never been published before. Perhaps only the photographer and certain editors had glanced at these "outtakes" before the plates were stored away in the Tower. So it's our pleasure to now share these visual documents of a crime boss known around the world.

—ROBIN DAUGHTRIDGE
ASSOCIATE MANAGING EDITOR / PHOTOGRAPHY AND VIDEO

ABOUT THE ARTICLES IN THIS BOOK

Throughout this book, actual text from historical *Chicago Tribune* articles is displayed. Though most articles do not appear in their entirety for space and content reasons, none of the historical text in this book has been altered in any way.

OCTOBER 1931

INTRODUCTION

In the three years I spent researching and writing my book about Al Capone, he came to me often in my dreams. Usually, he was smiling, friendly—perhaps a little too friendly. I felt as if he were trying to tell me he wasn't such a bad guy after all.

As you look through the pictures in this collection, you might begin to understand why Capone appeared that way in my dreams and also why reporters and business associates of Capone's in the 1920s were often surprised that the notorious gangster, known around the world as Scarface and Public Enemy Number One, was a surprisingly gregarious and easygoing fellow. Sometimes.

Make no mistake: Capone was a violent man. Though he was never convicted of a violent crime, there's good reason to believe he committed at least one or two murders with his own hands and sanctioned or ordered many more. He was a criminal operating a dizzying array of illegal enterprises, including speakeasies, brothels, and casinos. Yet Capone was also a savvy enough businessman to conduct many of these illegal activities in a public manner and to admit that he was providing "entertainment" to the people of Chicago.

To understand why this was possible, the modern American must understand at least a little bit of the culture created by Prohibition, a culture that managed to turn upside down many of the moral standards of the day. There was the sense in Chicago and all over the country that this law was wrong, and that the people circumventing it by supplying beer and whiskey were not criminals at all but heroes of a dirty sort. So it was not so preposterous for Capone to think that he was, in a way, living the American Dream. Granted, it was a bloodier version than most, but nevertheless Capone saw himself as an immigrant's kid trying to grab with both hands the opportunities offered by this great country, land of the free and home of the brave.

You can see that attitude in these photos. Look at how often he's seen smiling, even on trial for income tax evasion as he faces a stacked jury and prejudiced judge. Look at the confidence with which he faces crowds of gawkers. Look at the way he dresses: Capone was the inventor of gangster chic, a style that takes the banker's attire and blows it up with wider pinstripes, bolder colors, and more dashing accoutrements. Among friends, his nickname was Snorky, which was a term used at the time for a dandy dresser. Clearly, this was not a man who felt like a criminal on the run. Rather, Capone comes across in these images as confident and welcoming of the attention.

In the end, of course, this confidence is what did him in. The other gangsters never got him. The cops never got him. Capone was brought down largely by his hubris. By talking so freely with the press and by bragging about his illegal activities, he was essentially thumbing his nose at the federal government. And so while other bootleggers and gangsters went about their business with little or no scrutiny from the federal government, Capone incurred the wrath of none less than the President of the United States, Herbert Hoover. It was Hoover who gave the order to take Capone out of operation by any means possible, even if the best his men could do was to build a case for income tax evasion (for which Capone was indicted in 1931).

Capone should have seen it coming. But perhaps he was too busy worrying about his wardrobe.

—JONATHAN EIG
AUTHOR OF "GET CAPONE: THE SECRET PLOT THAT CAPTURED
AMERICA'S MOST WANTED GANGSTER."

STRIKE DOWN GANG RULE.

There are other criminals, but they are amateurs compared to the professional gangster. They are the apprentices of crime. They may work their way into a gang if they are successful enough. They are also the ones who get caught and are convicted.

It is the gangster who does not get caught or, if caught, escapes penalty.

The gangster is responsible for crime in Chicago. He does not commit it all, but it is he who sets the pace and the example.

OCTOBER 5, 1926

PART I

CAPONE: THE MAN AND HIS FAMILY

RAID 3 CAPONE HIDEAWAYS, BUT MISS GANG CHIEF

Raids in Berwyn Show Guards on Duty.

Three finely furnished homes in Berwyn were searched early yesterday morning for Al Capone, chief of the public enemies. Al was not there, but the searchers learned that the gang chieftain stopped occasionally at each of the places.

Well tailored clothing belonging to the bootleg king, for whom a vagrancy warrant has been unserved for several months, convinced the searchers they were on Capone's trail. Municipal Judge John H. Lyle, who issued the vagrancy warrant for Capone, was in the group seeking to serve it and he was accompanied by Chief Investiagor Pat Roche, Assistant State's Attorney Charles F. Rathbun and James E. McShane, and Special United States Intelligence Officer Clarence Converse.

Roche said it was apparent the gang chief was well guarded and the frequent changing of his places of abode was for his own protection from rival public enemies as well as to elude the police.

DECEMBER 1, 1930

1926
Ralph Sheldon (right) and Al Capone at a roadside bar in Tijuana, Mexico. Police discovered this photo during a raid on mob headquarters.

"YOU CAN ALL GO THIRSTY NOW," CAPONE GOOD-BY

Says He's Benefactor Who's Misrepresented.

Al Capone, also known as Al Brown, a chief among Chicago's providers of the forbidden vices—wine, revelry, and games of chance—announced last night from his headquarters at the Metropole hotel that he is going to leave this city high and dry.

"I'm leaving for St. Petersburg, Fla., tomorrow," Capone said. "Let the worthy citizens of Chicago get their liquor the best they can. I'm sick of the job—it's a thankless one and full of grief. I don't know when I'll get back, if ever. But it won't be until after the holidays, anyway."

Wears His Hunting Suit.

The high mogul of the Capone-Lombardo combination was sitting comfortably in an easy chair. He was clad in the ultranifty hunting suit he bought for his recent jaunt to the north woods. His jowls still carried the six day beard growth cultivated while he and his companions tramped after bear and deer and hare.

As he pursued his muse, Capone rather gently reproached the police, who accused him of being one of the principals of a syndicate which has been reaping profits of $75,000,000 annually in exploiting vice in Chicago.

"I've been spending the best years of my life as a public benefactor," he said. "I've given people the light pleasures, shown them a good time. And all I get is abuse—the existence of a hunted man. I'm called a killer.

Now Town Can Be Perfect.

"Well, tell the folks I'm going away now. I guess murder will stop. There won't be any more booze. You won't be able to find a crap game, even, let alone a roulette wheel or a faro game. I guess Mike Hughes won't need his 1,000 extra capos, after all.

"Public service is my motto. Ninety-nine per cent of the people in Chicago drink and gamble. I've tried to serve them decent liquor and square games. But I'm not appreciated. It's no use."

Why should he want to go to Florida, land of the rum runners, Capone was asked.

"I've got some property in St. Petersburg I want to sell," he said. "It's warm there, but not too warm.

Shame If He's Forgot.

"Say, the coppers won't have to lay all the gang murders on me now. Maybe they'll find a new hero for the headlines. It would be a shame, wouldn't it, if while I was away they would forget about me and find a new gangland chief?

"I wish all my friends and enemies Merry Christmas and a Happy New Year. That's all they'll get from me this year. I hope I don't spoil anybody's Christmas by not sticking around."

Then Capone forsook his humorous grin.

"My wife and my mother hear so much about what a terrible criminal I am. It's getting too much for them, and I'm just sick of it all myself."

Ousts Death Volunteer.

"The other day a man came in here and said that he had to have $3,000. If I'd give it to him, he said,

he would make be beneficiary in $15,000 insurance policy he'd ta[ke] out and then off himself. I had have him pushed out.

"Today I got a letter from woman in England. Even over the I'm known as a gorilla. She offer[ed] to pay my passage to London if I kill some neighbors she'd been ha[v]ing a quarrel with.

"The papers have made me o[ut] a millionaire, and hardly an ho[ur] goes by that somebody doesn't wa[nt] me to invest in some scheme o[r] stake somebody in business.

"That's what I've got to put wit[h] just because I give the public wh[at] the public wants. I never had to sen[d] out high pressure salesmen. Why, could never meet the demand!"

Proud of Lack of Record.

Forcefully the gangster declare[d] he never was convicted of a crim[e] in his life. He has no "record," as th[e] police call it.

"I never stuck up a man in m[y] life," he added. "Neither did an[y] of my agents ever rob anybody o[r] burglarize any homes while the[y] worked for me. They might hav[e] pulled plenty of jobs before the[y] came with me or after they le[ft] me, but not while they were in m[y] [unreadable]."

Then, Capone warmly indorse[d] [sic] Cicero, that village on th[e] southwest of Chicago, which ha[s] been pictured for years as th[e] cradle of the country's vice. Ther[e] for a long time Capone and Johnn[y] Torrio, his patron who broke hi[m] into the game, made a headquarter[s] from which to direct their vice an[d] booze and gambling traffic.

"Cicero is a city of 75,00[0] people, and the cleanest burg in th[e] U. S. A.," declared Capone, force[fully]. "There's only one gamblin[g]

MIAMI DESTINED TO BE RULED BY KING SCARFACE

Capone Making Things Hum at Winter Resort.

Capone's home is one of the most beautiful on Palm Island. Surrounded by a gang of strong arms, it is far more peaceful than any spot he could find in Chicago.

Scarface is a smart man and a business man, Miamians have found out. This part of the country is wide open, they insist. All sorts of liquor are immediately available, from beer to champagne.

FEBRUARY 28, 1929

1929
Capone (in a bathing suit) at his vacation home in Miami, Florida.

This photo was retouched prior to publication; Capone's outline has been darkened for more definition. Because presses couldn't reproduce photographic images well, definition was often added to more clearly see differences between similarly colored backgrounds (i.e., a white form against a sky, a suit against a dark wall).

Undated photo

RALPH CAPONE'S IN AGAIN, IF THAT MEANS ANYTHING

Gangster Faces New Gun Charge, but—

Last Thursday Lieut. Albert Hoffman and his detective bureau squad spotted Ralph and a pair driving by at Wabash avenue and 22d street. They made a break to escape, but the traffic light stopped them at Michigan avenue, and meanwhile the detectives had turned their car about and were pulling alongside....

All three were charged with vagrancy and release on bail....

Deputy Commissioner Stege asked Capone why he carried the weapons.

Guarding His Pay Roll

"I'm in the furniture business in Cicero," was the reply. "These men work for me. We carry large amounts of money to pay our employees, and we carried the guns to protect the money."

"What were you doing in Chicago, then?" Deputy Stege demanded to know.

"O, I was coming to have dinner with my wife," Capone said.

OCTOBER 7, 1928

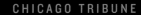

Prepare Feast for Capone's Return

GANG LEADER'S KIN EXPECT HIM BACK TUESDAY

Philadelphia Eager to Be Rid of Him.

Festive preparations for the return of the titular head of the House of Capone were observed last night in the neighborhood of 7244 South Prairie avenue, where the mother, brother and sister of Chicago's gangster chief, "Scarface Al," live comfortably in a two apartment building. Al is due home on Tuesday.

CONTINUED ON PAGE 18

MARCH 16, 1930

FEBRUARY 1930
Home of Al Capone, 7244 South Prairie Avenue, in the Park Manor neighborhood of Chicago.

"Say, I won't tell you anything."

CONTINUED FROM PAGE 17

Last night visitors at the Capone home were answered, through a thick oaken door, by Ralph Capone Jr., 12 years old.

"Where's grandma?" he was asked. "Out," was the guarded reply. A bag of candy was rattled enticingly and the door swung open.

"Is grandma going to have a special kind of spaghetti for Uncle Al's dinner?"

"Yea, walnut flavored, probably," was the reply. More questions—few answers. Finally this from the small, overalled figure:

"Say, I won't tell you anything. Another paper sent some people out here to play marbles with me. I won 90 cents from them and didn't tell them a thing." The door closed.

MARCH 16, 1930

FEBRUARY 24, 1930
Another view of Al Capone's home.

SISTER OF CAPONE, HIS CHIEF DEFENDER, EAGERLY AWAITS HIM

Whatever others may say of Al Capone's well known past and uncertain future, he has one loyal friend who believes him incapable of wrong doing. That is Capone's sister, Mafalda, 19 years old, a girl with laughing gray eyes fringed with curling black lashes. Mafalda is waiting for her brother with a pounding heart and full larder.

Not sure of the hour when Capone will arrive, Mafalda, her aged grandmother, Theresa, and her 12 year old nephew, Ralph Capone Jr., whose father is waiting for Uncle Al in Philadelphia, are tremulously preparing the turkeys for a homecoming feast. The three live together at 7244 Prairie avenue, while Al's wife and mother are at his Miami estate.

"Why do people care about us?" Mafalda asked yesterday. "I don't see why the newspapers put headlines in about my brother. I wish they would say how good he is. Every one who really knows him says it."

MARCH 17, 1930

MARCH 24, 1930
The alley behind Al Capone's home.

1930
Al Capone and his mother, Teresa.

MARCH 28, 1930
Capone on the move.

**CAPONE'S YOUNGER BROTHER SEIZED BY PO-
LICE.** Matthew Capone, 21 years old, who says he is student
at Villa Nova college in Pennsylvania, at police station before
release on bonds of $150 cash.
[TRIBUNE Photo.]

A raid upon the home of Al Capone at 7244 Prairie avenue resulted in the arrest of Matthew, 21 year old brother of Al, when he drove his automobile up to the door. Neither the notorious gang leader nor his brother Ralph, both named as two of the 26 public enemies in the crime commission's list, were in the home.

Young Capone said he had returned but recently from Villa Nova college in Pennsylvania, where he was a student, and that he knew nothing of his brothers' whereabouts. He was held in a cell until Attorney Thomas Nash appeared with a petition for a writ of habeas corpus before Judge Joseph Sabath. The police then agreed to book Capone on a charge of driving a car without an Illinois license or city vehicle tag. He was released last night after he had posted a $150 cash bond.

SEPTEMBER 19, 1930

SEPTEMBER 1930
Matthew Capone, Al's brother, is taken into custody by acting lieutenant Frank Aldenhover, reportedly on charges of having improper (Pennsylvania) license plates.

HUSH, HUSH.

New York is continuing to reap the consequences of the hush-hush policy which has hid so long the gang rule, crime, and corruption this press has advertised as peculiar belongings of Chicago…

Of course, we too have our hushers. One of them has sent us a protest against the publication of a photograph of Capone at the Cubs-Sox game, with the suggestion that it is evidence of an unscrupulous disregard of the public interest on the part of the newspapers and a bad example for the young. The intelligence of this protest is given special emphasis by the fact that Capone was at this time reported to be the object of vigorous but unavailing search by the police. To our benighted mind this exposure of Capone at the ball game was a public service, but the hushers do not see it that way. Fortunately Chicago is not afraid to face the truth, and the winning fight it is making against crime and corruption is sufficient proof for all but the hushers that its candor and courage pay.

SEPTEMBER 14, 1931

SEPTEMBER 14, 1931
Capone (first row, third from left).

1931
Al Capone talks with the Chicago Cubs' Gabby Hartnett at Comiskey
Park. Capone's son is seated between him and State Representative
Roland Libonati. Behind Capone is "Machine Gun" Jack McGurn
(face hidden) and two bodyguards.

OCTOBER 1931

OCTOBER 1931

oto

Ralph Capone and 9 Seized for Beer Quiz

Ralph Capone, brother of Al Capone, and nine other men were seized yesterday by police from the state's attorney' office in a raid on a flat above a tavern in Berwyn. They were questioned concerning complaints made to the state's attorney that Capone had reorganized the remnants of his brother's old gang to force saloonkeepers in the western part of Cook county to buy the beer of the Great Lakes brewery of Calumet City.

G. Konvalinka

As the police were taking their prisoners to the street they saw Capone running down the alley and captured him. He denied that he was in the beer business. He said he had been playing golf and had stopped in at the tavern for a glass of beer.

[Republican Committeeman] Konvalinka said that Capone had merely "happened to drop in" at the flat just before the police arrived. Capone gave his address as 7244 Prairie avenue and his occupation as a homeowner.

AUGUST 23, 1934

1934
Ralph Capone, brother of Al Capone, after being questioned by lawmen regarding "forced beer sales."

DECEMBER 20, 1950
Ralph Capone appears before the Kefauver committee in Chicago. The Kefauver committee, formally known as the Special Committee to Investigate Organized Crime in Interstate Commerce, was created in 1950 by the United States Senate to investigate organized crime that crossed state borders.

Kefauver to Give City Fu

Testimony of Police Captains

O'Connor to Study Facts on Income, Possible Action

Sen. Kefauver asserted that despite the fact that many witnesses were not heard, the testimony actually obtained demonstrates that "interstate crime, to a great degree," centers in Chicago.

CONTINUED ON PAGE 40

CONTINUED FROM PAGE 39

GANG LEADERS MISSING

Among the witnesses unheard, in addition to the police captains, were the top men of the Capone syndicate, such as Tony Accardo, Jack Guzik, and the Fischetti brothers, whom the committee's subpoena servers have been unable to find. Kefauver said that it may be necessary for the committee to return for additional hearings or that some of the remaining witnesses may be questioned at hearings elsewhere. He said the committee staff will remain here for several days.

"Some of the evidence produced should be sufficient for local authorities to begin investigations of their own," he said.

Witnesses before the committee yesterday included William Johnston, president of Sportsman's park; Hugo Bennett, former auditor at the track; Ralph and Jon Capone, brothers of Al Capone; Johnny Patton, aging boy mayor of Burnham, and Thomas J Cawley, operator of gambling houses in La Salle and Streator.

JOHN CAPONE COMPLAINS

John Capone, 46, and slightly bald, complained to the committee that the reason he can't find legitimate employment is because of his name, altho he has changed his name to John Martin, "and this situation is not making matters any better."

The committee appeared to be intrigued by John's bookkeeping methods. He has only one item of income on his income tax return —"miscellaneous."

Q.—What is the source of your income? A.—I am a speculator.

Q.—What do you speculate in? A.—I would rather not answer that question for fear it might tend to incriminate me.

Q.—Are you a gambler? A.—I am, yes sir.

Q.—What do you gamble on? A.—I gamble on whatever I think I have a chance on.

Q.—Do you gamble on the horses? A.—Yes sir.

He said he once bought some stock in the Steelco company, a drilling concern in Wyoming, but never got any dividends.

He said that when he makes out his income tax return, he just takes a figure out of his head and gives it to an accountant, and the accountant puts it down as miscellaneous.

Q.—How do you arrive at that lump sum? A.—Well, I just keep track of it.

Q.—How do you keep track of it? A.—Well, if I win any money today, and I win the next day, I forget about the first day; and just keep track of the total balance.

Q.—How do you do that? A.—In my mind.

He said he has a bank account and a safe deposit box, but refused to say how much he has in either.

RALPH CAPONE ANNOYED

John's brother, Ralph [Bottles] Capone, expressed annoyance when committee counsel referred to the Capone gang. He said he never knew of any Capone gang.

He said he makes $3,000 a year as manager of the Rex hotel in Mercer, Wis., and he also has an income of $18,000 a year from an interest in a cigaret vending machine business at 4831 Cermak rd.

Ralph spoke in a soft voice.

He said he never had any direct connection with the activities of his brother, Al, during prohibition.

Never Questioned Brother

Q.—What was Al's business? A.—I never asked him.

He said he never lived in the Lexington hotel, which Al used as a headquarters, but that he was acquainted with Johnny Patton, the boy mayor of Burnham; Rocco de Grazio, the Fischettis, Tough Tony Capezio, and Jack Guzik.

He denied any connection with gambling in Chicago, except as a patron of gambling houses, observing that "I'd like to have the money I lost in Chicago gambling houses."

DECEMBER 21, 1950

NOVEMBER 21, 1952

Ralph J. Capone (left) after Judge William J. Campbell dismissed his income-tax case. Ralph is shown with his lawyer, George Callaghan.

LASHES CAPONE, VOIDS CHARGE OF TAX EVASION

Court Decides Note Protected Hoodlum

Capone, in court with his attorney, George F. Callaghan, commented after the hearing, "Like I said last year, all I did was make an honest effort to settle the darn thing."

NOVEMBER 22, 1952

PART II

CAPONE AND THE LAW

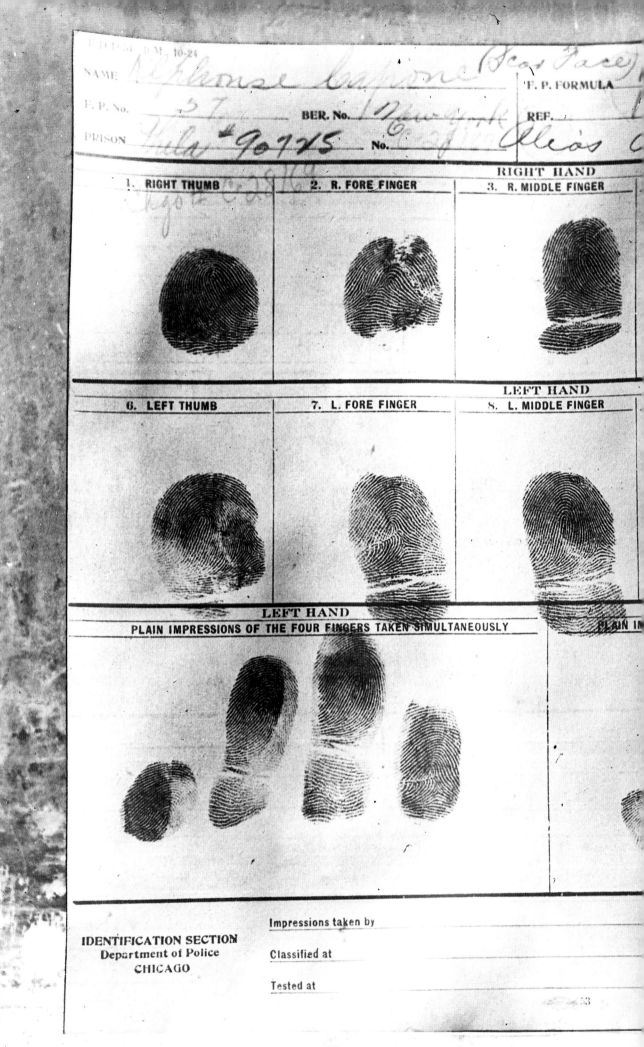

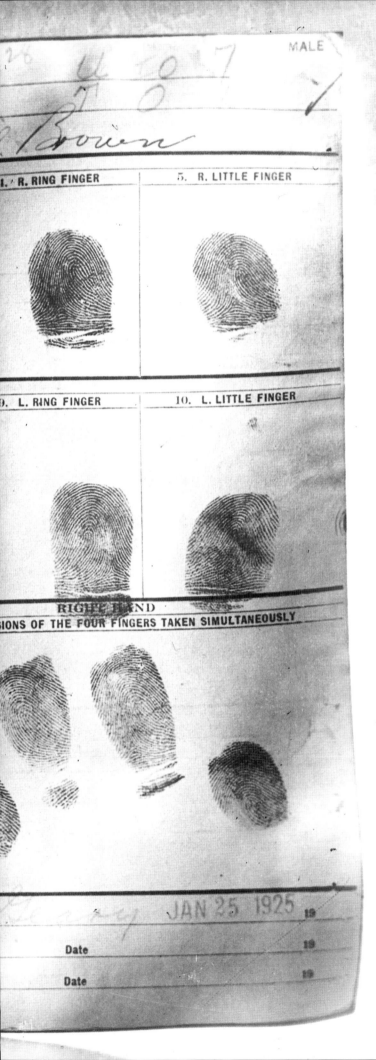

MALE

2. Bowen

4. R. RING FINGER | 5. R. LITTLE FINGER

9. L. RING FINGER | 10. L. LITTLE FINGER

RIGHT HAND

IMPRESSIONS OF THE FOUR FINGERS TAKEN SIMULTANEOUSLY

JAN 25 1925 19

Date 19

Date 19

TORRIO IS SHOT; POLICE HUNT FOR O'BANION MEN

Rum Czar's Driver Is Also Hit.

Torrio attended O'Banion's wake. His presence was interrupted by the underworld as a warning to any who challenged him that they might expect to sleep in silver-bronze caskets surrounded by thousands of dollars worth of flowers.

But Torrio's enemies were not cowed. A week ago they tried to assassinate his first lieutenant, Al Capone.

That attempt failed. Yesterday three of them lay in wait for half an hour opposite the Torrio home, waiting for Torrio to return. At 4:30 o'clock Torrio and his wife, Anna, drove up in a heavy sedan. While one of the gunmen remained at the wheel, the other two jumped out and shot Torrio, who tried to escape by running into the apartment building. The attackers leaped back into their machine and fled.

Capone was finally taken into custody for questioning. The police admitted he had revealed nothing to them.

JANUARY 25, 1925

JANUARY 25, 1925
Al Capone's fingerprints.

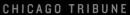

CAPONE, 4 AIDS FINED $2,601 IN JOLIET COURTS

Plead Guilty on Charges of Carrying Guns.

Al Capone, Chicago gang leader, and four of his lieutenants pleaded guilty to charges of gun toting in two court appearances in Joliet last night and paid maximum fines amounting to $2,601.15.

In addition a Joliet street corner Santa Claus of the Salvation Army clanged his bell with renewed vigor while fingering a crisp new $10 note that Capone dropped with a characteristic flourish into his alms kettle.

Both the court cases had been continued from last Friday when Capone stepped off a Santa Fé train from California at Joliet only to fall into the hands of Chief of Police John Corcoran. The gang leader and four of his henchmen who had motored to Joliet to meet him were all found by the chief to be armed with automatics.

DECEMBER 23, 1927

DECEMBER 30, 1927
Joliet Police Chief John Corcoran and the guns he confiscated from Capone and his gang when they got off the train in Joliet, Illinois.

MARCH 19, 1929

Capone, left, and First Deputy Police Commissioner John Stege. This photo was taken a day before Capone began his testimony in front of a federal grand jury regarding the St. Valentine's Day Massacre. After a week of testimony, on March 27, 1929, Capone was arrested for contempt of court as he exited the courtroom. The contempt charge alleged that he had feigned illness to avoid appearing in court for a separate case that involved violating Prohibition laws.

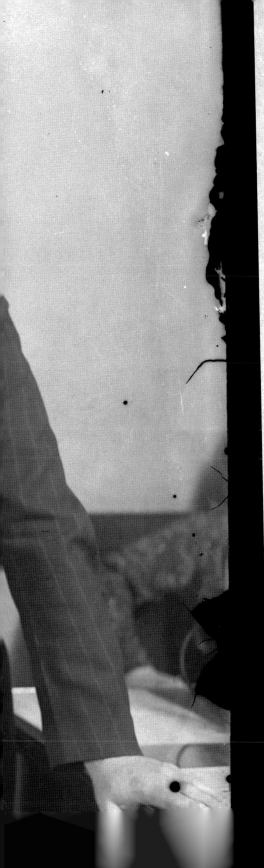

CAPONE TO FACE U. S. JURY, BUT HE FEARS CITY COPS

Also He Wants Immunity on Federal Charge.

Alphonse Capone is scheduled to appear before the federal grand jury tomorrow morning to answer questions about booze and gangs in Chicago. There was a rumor in the underworld last night that Capone had arrived in Chicago, having made the trip from his Miami estate by automobile. Other reports were that he was on his way. Just what will happen when Capone appears before the jury is problematical.

When Mr. Capone is summoned for questioning there promises to be a hub-bub unless the gang leader is granted immunity from prosecution for what he tells. His attorneys were firm on that point yesterday. Further they demanded that, since their client is a federal witness, the government must protect him from any efforts of the police to cart him off to the detective bureau for a quizzing on the Moran massacre.

"The government called Capone from his legal residence in Florida to appear before the grand jury," said Attorneys William F. Waugh and Benjamin Epstein, "and it will have to give him its protection until he is safely at home again. Also, Capone will not sign an immunity waiver and won't answer questions at all unless they assure him he won't be indicted for what he says."

MARCH 19, 1929

pg. 3

CAPONE, AS U. S. WITNESS, SHUNS HIS OLD HAUNTS

Crowd Jams Streets to See Gang Chief.

Alphonse Capone held the attention of Chicago for a few hours yesterday, but as daylight and limelight faded he became an outcast. Last night he was in hiding, said to be unwelcome even in his own home town of Cicero which was waiting for its latest saloon killing to be forgotten.

Capone arrived amid the tumult of crowds, but he came only because the United States government had sternly commanded his presence here. He testified before the federal grand jury, held at least fifty persons waiting in a stuffy corridor for more than an hour while he was in the jury room, and caused policemen to be required as guards and traffic managers around the Federal building all day. Then the gang chieftain departed to join those of his bodyguard who are in

MARCH 20, 1929
A crowd gathered outside the
Chicago Federal Building, waiting
for Al Capone to exit after his first
day of testimony before a federal
grand jury.

U.S. CITES CAPONE FOR CONTEMPT; DOUBTS 'ILLNESS'

Warrant Served After 2d Grand Jury Quiz.

Alphonse Capone of Cicero and Miami became involved in his first serious trouble with the federal government yesterday when a warrant was served upon him charging contempt of court, which, if the charges are proved, can send the racketeer to jail for one year, plus a $1,000 fine. Behind the warrant lurks the figure of Assistant Attorney General Mabel Willebrandt.

Capone now stands accused of faking illness to avoid appearing before the federal grand jury. A subpoena, issued on Feb. 21, commanded him to present himself in Chicago on March 12. On March 9 Attorneys William F. Waugh and Ben Epstein petitioned Judge James H. Wilkerson to stay the return of Capone for thirty days. He was very ill, they said, and waved a long letter in which the gangster claimed he had been stricken by bronchial pneumonia and had been incapacitated from Jan. 13 to Feb. 23. He was feeble and convalescing, the letter stated. The court granted a delay of eight days.

The gangster was hustled downstairs to the office of the clerk of the United States District court, where he made his bond of $5,000, and left the building.

MARCH 28, 1929

U. S. SUMMONS AL CAPONE TO COURT MONDAY

Gang Leader Must Face Contempt Charge.

"The presence of Al Capone is urgently requested at 10 o'clock Monday morning, Dec. 15, before Federal Judge James H. Wilkerson in the federal building at Chicago."

This firm invitation was issued yesterday by United States District Attorney George E. Q. Johnson. It was a surprise to gangdom because the word had begun to spread that Capone, known as public enemy No. 1, had, in some fashion, gained immunity from the concerted attacks of law enforcement officials upon hoodlums in Chicago.

His Lawyer In a Quandary.

Inasmuch as Capone's address is at present unknown, the summons was presented to his attorney, Benjamin P. Epstein, who promptly demanded:

"How in hell can I get him in court by Monday? I don't know where he is."

"Maybe," he added hopefully. "This only means that his attorney should appear."

But Johnson, apprised of this utterance, declared firmly:

"It means that Capone, in person, must be present in court."

Capone was cited for contempt of court two years ago for failure to submit to questioning before a federal grand jury in connection with the investigation of the Chicago Heights liquor ring. He has been at liberty under a bond of $5,000 pending this trial. Since then he has served a year's jail sentence at Philadelphia for carrying concealed weapons.

DECEMBER 13, 1930

MARCH 21, 1930
Al Capone in front of the
Detective Bureau.

FEBRUARY 2, 1931
Al Capone in the Chicago Chief of
Detectives' office.

1931
Al Capone's
booking mug.

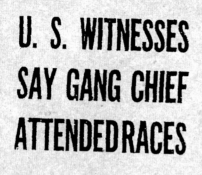

CK' CAPONE'S JAUNTS TOLD

U. S. WITNESSES SAY GANG CHIEF ATTENDED RACES

Makes Defense in Court Today.

FEBRUARY 26, 1931

FEBRUARY 25, 1931
Al Capone in the Chicago
criminal courthouse.

Crowds See Al Capone on Trial in Federal

Court on Contempt Charge and Taken to Detective Bureau as Vagrant

[Sketch by Tribune artist.]

COURTROOM CROWDED AS GOVERNMENT PRESENTS ITS CASE AGAINST AL CAPONE IN CONTEMPT OF COURT PROCEEDINGS.
(1) Al Capone, (2) Benjamin P. Epstein, and (3) William F. Waugh, Capone's attorneys; (4) Jacob Grossman, assistant United States district attorney, questioning (5) W. R. Foster, Hialeah, Fla., government witness; (6) Judge James H. Wilkerson. The room was filled to capacity, spectators occupying the jury box in the background.

(Story on page 1.)

CAPONE TO JAIL

Al Capone, sentenced to six months in jail by Federal Judge Wilkerson for contempt of court, had taken a casual but characteristic attitude toward judicial process....

He had learned from his operations in Chicago that he was a part of government under reciprocating arrangements in which for value received he conducted certain enterprises requiring political protection and occasional murder. His experience in Philadelphia, where he went to jail for a year for carrying a gun, would not destroy his confidence in the general dependability of the system. That was a jam in which he was careless in unorganized territory. It was an exceptional event.

MARCH 2, 1931

pg. 8

CAPONE OBJECTS TO 'SCARFACE' IN WARRANT; WINS

Vagrancy Trial Is Set for March 20.

Al Capone, who heads the public enemy list, made a brief stop in Judge Frank M. Padden's Felony court yesterday to object to the designation of himself as "Scarface Al" in the pending vagrancy warrant, which was issued by Judge John. H. Lyle when he presided over that court. Attorney Michael Ahern, representing Capone, succeeded in soothing his client's feeling by getting the phrase stricken from the warrant.

"Alphonse Capone is this man's right name," said Attorney Ahern as he stepped up to the court rail with his client in response to the announcement from the clerk of the "People of the State of Illinois against Al Capone, alias Scarface Al Brown."

"I ask that the epithet 'Scarface Al,' which appears on this complaint, be stricken from the record," continued Attorney Ahern while Capone vigorously nodded his approval.

"I'm going to file a new complaint anyway and I will leave the epithet as you call it off the sheet," replied Prosecutor Ditchburne.

MARCH 5, 1031

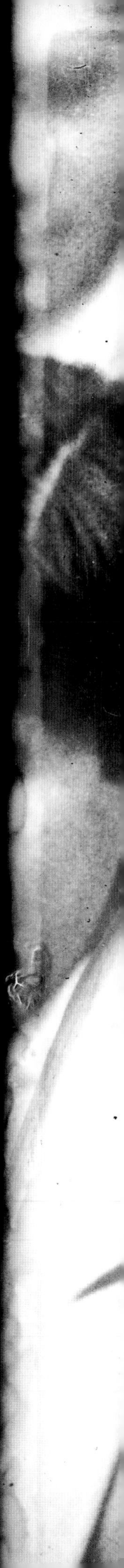

Undated photo

MARCH 9, 1931
Al Capone leaving the Chicago
Federal Building.

MARCH 9, 1931
Al Capone leaving the
Chicago Federal Building.

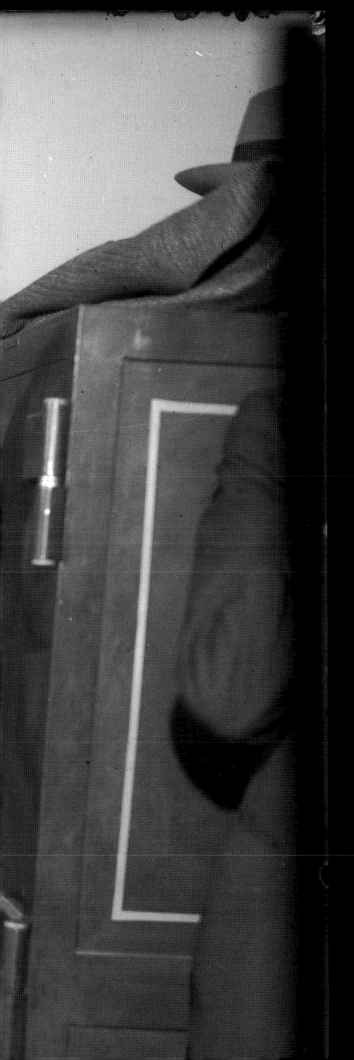

MARCH 10, 1931
Al Capone and Assistant State's
Attorney Frank Mast.

MARCH 21, 1931
Crowds at the Chicago Federal
Building for Al Capone's trial.

MARCH 22, 1931
Al Capone enters his car (left) in the
courtyard of the criminal court building
after appearing in felony court.

[TRIBUNE Photo.]

FREED BECAUSE NO POLICEMAN KNOWS ABOUT HIM. Al Capone, gang chief, who was discharged by Judge Padden when police failed to produce vagrancy evidence. The sneer on his face gives him an unusually ferocious expression.

CAPONE VAGRANT CASE DROPPED; LACK EVIDENCE

(Picture on back page.)

Assistant State's Attorney Harry Ditchburne told Judge Frank Padden in the Felony court yesterday that he was unable to find any policemen who could give evidence of illegal activities of Al Capone, public enemy No. 1, within the last 13 months. The prosecutor said he therefore must ask for the dismissal of the vagrancy charge against Capone and the court allowed the order to be entered.

APRIL 4, 1931

APRIL 4, 1931
Al Capone, Assistant State's
Attorney Frank Mast and Bailiff
Joe Weinberg in a Chicago Federal
Building courtroom.

Assistant State's Attorney
Harry Ditchburne, left, and
Al Capone in a Chicago
courtroom (undated photo).

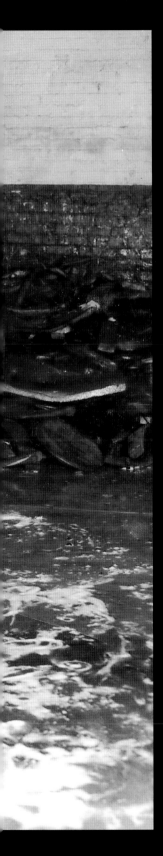

CAPONE BREWERY RUNNING ONLY 5 DAYS IS RAIDED

Destroy Plant and Beer Worth $100,000.

A Capone brewery at 3156 South Wabash avenue, with beer worth $75,000 at the standard retail price, and physical equipment valued at $25,000, was raided early yesterday by special prohibition agents under Chief W. E. Bennett. The plant had been in operation only five days.

Raid on "Smell" Affidavit.

The equipment included two electric beer pumps, an air compressor, fourteen 2,500 gallon tanks and five 1,800 gallon cooling tanks.

There was an electric blower to force the fumes out through the roof and over the heads of chance snoopers, and moth balls were strewn around the doors and windows to counteract the beer odor. Even these precautions were futile, for the search warrant issued by United States Commissioner Walker was based on a "smell" affidavit.

APRIL 12, 1931

APRIL 1931

Federal agents seize and destroy 1 of 115 barrels of beer in raid on a brewery on South Wabash Avenue.

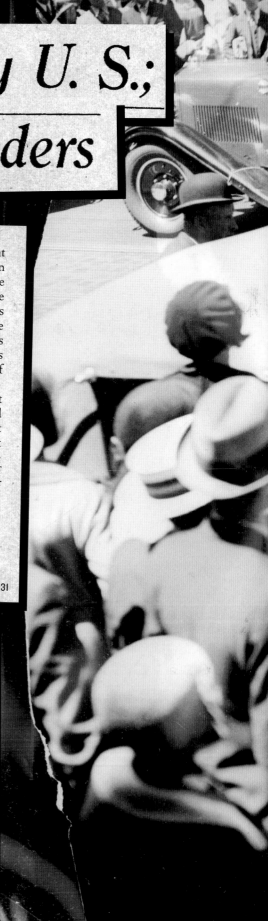

Capone Indicted by U. S.; Surrenders

GANGSTER GIVES $50,000 BOND IN TAX FRAUD CASE

Accused of Evading $215,080 Levy.

A day of reckoning arrived yesterday for Scarface Alphonse Capone, public enemy No. 1. He surrendered to the government after having been named in an indictment returned early in the afternoon which accused him of evasion of income taxes amounting to $215,080. United State Attorney George E. Q. Johnson, who has won a conviction against every gangster he has tried for income tax frauds, announced he was ready for the supreme test against Capone, the chief of gang chiefs.

The government alleged that Capone owes taxes of $215,080 on a net income of $1,038,654 for the years 1924 to 1929, inclusive. The government does not say that this was the total of Capone's income of those six years, but it represents the amount the government expects to be able to prove that the chief gangster pocketed.

The statement was made that during those six years Capone filed no income tax return, although it was known that he received a vast income, due to his monopoly of the booze, alky, and beer business of the Chicago territory, his control of the gambling rackets and his profits from his string of brothels. Capone had boasted that he was too smart for the government, that he put no money in banks and no money could be traced to him.

JUNE 6, 1931

JUNE 1931
Al Capone arriving at the Chicago Federal Building, surrounded by police to prevent any disturbance. Capone is in front of the cab door with a cigar in his mouth.

Al Capone in Hands
of Judge Today

CHIEF OF GANGS WAITS DECISION ON PRISON TERM

Sentence to Follow Final U. S. Evidence.

The fate of Al Capone will rest today with Federal Judge James H. Wilkerson, who will decide on the length of the prison term the gang leader must serve at Leavenworth on his please of guilty to two indictments....

Capone has pleaded guilty to eight counts of violating the income tax laws in attempting to evade payment of $215,080 on an income of $1,038,000 over a five year period, and to a blanket conspiracy charge in connection with his reputed $20,000,000 a year beer business.

JULY 30, 1931

JULY 1931

Al Capone waits for a sentencing decision from Judge James H. Wilkerson on charges of defrauding the government and violating Prohibition.

The photographer in the background holds a typical press camera of the day, which used 4-by-5-inch glass plates.

JULY 1931

SMILE FADES FROM GANG CHIEFTAIN'S FACE AS JUDGE BLASTS HIS HOPE OF BEING GIVEN SHORT TERM IN PRISON. At the left is Al Capone, his face wearing a smile similar to the one which appeared upon it as he entered court. At the right is Capone as he appeared after the smile faded from his face when he realized his predicament. In the center is Judge James H. Wilkerson, wearing the stern expression he assumed when he announced he could not be a party to any agreement with Public Enemy No. 1.   [TRIBUNE Photo.]   (Story on page 1.)

CAPONE 'DEAL' RULING TODAY

JUDGE REFUSES TO BE BOUND TO EASY SENTENCE

Gangster Seeks to Drop Guilty Plea.

The gangster's hopes of escaping with a two or three year sentence through an arrangement with the government were shattered, and his attorneys quickly moved to change their pleas from guilty to not guilty on the income tax evasion and booze conspiracy indictments against Capone, who is No. 1 on the list of public enemies.

The motion to back out on the pleas of guilty, which can be done only with the court's permission, was continued for consideration until 2 p. m. today, when the judge will rule as to whether Capone may withdraw his plea and go to trial or be sentenced on his plea as it stands.

Capone Stalks Into Court.

The porcine Capone stalked into the courtroom at 10 o'clock in the morning, beaming with the visible assurance that "everything was all set," that the prosecutors would say a few words to the court and he would be sentenced on the terms which he had accepted to plead guilty.

The arrogant manner had gone when the gangster slipped stealthily away with his attorneys at 3 o'clock in the afternoon. The collar that had been white and fresh in the morning was wilted, and his greasy hair was disarranged by the nervous mopping of his brow during the colloquy at the bar. The ear to ear grin was displaced by a sullen countenance as he slunk from the courtroom at the conclusion of the afternoon session.

JULY 31, 1931

CALL CAPONE
JURORS TODAY

U. S. CLEARS WAY
FOR TAX FRAUD
CASE TOMORROW

Gang Trial to Draw
Eyes of Nation.

The attention of the country will be commanded tomorrow by the trial of Al Capone as an income tax evader, which beings in Federal Judge James H. Wilkerson's court at 10 a.m. It will be the most famous of all the prosecutions of gang chieftains produced by the Volstead era and comparable in interest to the Loeb-Leopold trial.

Federal prosecutors headed by United States Attorney George E. Q. Johnson completed their preparations for the trial Saturday night, ending three years of unrelenting investigation born of a zeal to rid Chicago of its foremost public enemy. Seventy-five witnesses are under subpoena to give evidence of Capone's alleged $1,038,654 booze, gambling and vice income over a six year period, on which he paid no taxes.

OCTOBER 5, 1931

OCTOBER 6, 1931
Crowds gathering around the
Chicago Federal Building on the
first day of the Al Capone trial.

JURY IS CHOSEN IN OPENING DAY OF GANG TRIAL

Only One Chicagoan to Vote on Verdict.

Al Capone's celebrated bout with the federal government over the matter of his neglected income tax opened before Judge James H. Wilkerson yesterday in a speedy and orderly manner.

Attorney Michael Ahern, representing the gangland chief, objected to the swearing of the jury because it had been developed during examination that nine of them had served before on grand or petit juries in the federal courts. Judge Wilkerson overturned this objection without comment....

As the jury selection proceeded it became a struggle between the Capone attorneys, who preferred men closer to the metropolitan atmosphere, and the federal attorneys, who produced a line of retired farmers. At one time there were five farmers in the box, but this number was whittled down to one by the defense tactics. Only one Chicagoan is on the jury.

OCTOBER 7, 1931

OCTOBER 13, 1931
The jury for Al Capone's tax evasion trial.

SARNOFF-IRVING QUALITY HATS

HATS CLEANED - SUITS PRESSED

1931
Al Capone's trial jurors on
their way to lunch.

pg. 1

CAPONE'S TRAIL OF GOLD TRACED IN LUXURY SALES

$12,500 for an Auto; $30 for a Shirt.

From all the testimony of Capone's spending methods given yesterday and on previous days, it appears that he never had more than a few thousand dollars at a time, but that this came with weekly regularity. He often made deposits of a few hundreds and came in the next week to pay the balance. His tastes grew more expensive and his income evidently larger during the last three years.

Expenditures aggregating $40,000 during 1927, 1928, and 1929, were shown yesterday by the government. The prosecution even detailed Capone's underwear styles, his gifts of match lighters, and diamond belt buckles, his taste in furniture and decorations. His favorite colors, it appeared, are green and canary, and he has a decided notion of his own about house decorations.

Capone listened rather wearily to all these personal disclosures, and his attorneys were frankly uninterested.

"I don't even care enough to object," said Attorney Albert Fink, when the prosecutor showed the jurors one of 30 diamond belt buckles which Capone had purchased for $275 each.

OCTOBER 13, 1931

[TRIBUNE Photo.]

DIAMOND BUCKLES FIGURE IN TRIAL. One of jeweled belt buckles given away by Capone to friends. They figured in the testimony yesterday.

1931
Al Capone, center, in federal court in Chicago during his tax evasion trial, with lawyers Michael Ahern, left, and Albert Fink.

Al Capone leaving the Chicago
Federal Building (undated photo).

A crowd waits outside as Al Capone is scheduled to leave the Federal Building (undated photo).

Crowds wait outside the Chicago Federal Building for Al Capone's trial (undated photo).

U. S. May Place Al Capone in Cell Pending His Appeal

Al Capone's immediate freedom will be in the balance on Friday when his attorneys appear before Federal Judge James H. Wilkerson with motions to combat his conviction for income tax fraud. The date of the hearing, originally set for this morning, was advanced yesterday when Defense Counsel Michael Ahern asked more time for preparation.

That Capone's troubles are mounting was shown yesterday with the report that more grand jury testimony will be taken on the booze conspiracy indictment, charging him and 68 others with more than 5,000 violations of the prohibition law....

Capone's bodyguard, Philip D'Andrea, was taken before Judge Wilkerson yesterday morning on his contempt charge for carrying a pistol in the courtroom during the income tax trial.

OCTOBER 20, 1931

CAPONE SENTENCED.

Judge Wilkerson has sentenced Al Capone to 11 years' imprisonment and imposed a fine of $50,000. Before 1920 Capone was only Scarface Brown, known as one of the shady characters familiar to the vice districts of great communities, where profits came from gambling, drink and prostitution. Drinks could be sold legally then. The other profitable enterprises needed political protection. Brown evidently had abilities above the average in the muck of vice mongers, but abilities which required more opportunities than they found until the United States government, which has sent him to prison, offered them. They were called national prohibition.

Under prohibition Brown soon felt important enough to revert to his family name, Capone, and soon he had made that name a word which contained compendiously the whole new phenomenon of lawlessness in the country. He became the symbol of the gang, of the new verboten and its consequences, of a savage and startling criminality. He was a direct product of federal legislation.

Now the government which made Capone the symbol of everything wild and predatory in American life is punishing him, but not, however, for any of the criminality for which he stands in general report and common belief. He is punished quite candidly because he did not give the government its share of the earnings....

For Capone, to explain this carelessness, it was suggested that naïvely he did not think the profits made by violating laws were taxable; that it was ridiculous to make a report of such earning and offer the government a percentage. More likely the income tax law was just another one to be pushed over, but whatever Capone's ideas were, the issue the government made in these tax suits was simply that the gangster did not pay on what he made in lawlessness. There are other indictments against him charging the violations themselves, but the case today is one involving only his pecuniary infidelity to the government which, with its Volstead act, made him what he was before he was brought to trail. Ingratitude, you might call it.

OCTOBER 26, 1931

OCTOBER 16, 1931
Crowd waiting on Clark Street to see Al Capone during his trial.

CHICAGO PUBLIC ENEMY NO. 1 NOW CONVICT 40886

Gates at Atlanta Close on Capone.

Capone entered at 8:10 p.m., Chicago daylight time, accompanied by United States Marshal H.C.W. Laubenheimer. They walked up the stone steps to the outer gates between the tall Doric pillars, and the keeper within called out:

"Who are you?"

"The United States marshal from Chicago, bringing Alphonse Capone, a prisoner," said the marshal. The gates opened and Capone, trembling with emotion but silent, was taken to the second entrance gate, thirty feet back. Here Warden A. C. Aderhold met them. He shook hands with the marshal and then turned to Capone.

"What's your name?" he asked.

"Alphonse Capone," said the ex-gang chief, his voice broken and scarcely audible.

"What's your sentence?"

"Eleven years," said Capone in a mournful tone that suggested eternity.

In the receiving or dressing-in room, prison attachés explained, Capone's $125 custom tailored blue suit was exchanged for a suit of blue denim with his new distinguishing numeral—the only name he now has—stitched across the back of the jumper and the legs of the overalls. The things he brought down in the grip, linen and toilet articles, were checked, and Capone was taken to the quarantine section, where he will remain for a week or more.

His demeanor as he entered the prison was in sharp contrast to the defiant, grinning cheerfulness he maintained on the Dixie Flyer from Chicago. He was pale of face and walked unsteadily and the wisecracks were missing....

Vito Morici, Capone's companion on the journey and upper berth fellow, with whom he was handcuffed and leg-ironed during such sleep as they got, bade him good-by just as they left the train. He was taken to the city jail by a local deputy marshal for the night, and today he will go on to Florida for trial on a dyer act charge. Capone wished him luck as they parted....

"I hope the warden likes spaghetti," he said.

MAY 5, 1932

1932

Al Capone in a Pullman railroad car on his way to prison in Atlanta, Georgia, after a prolonged court battle. At right is H.C.W. Laubenheimer, the U.S. marshal who accompanied Capone to prison.

Capone's Companion on Prison Trip Back Home

Victor Morici, 18 years old, who rode from Chicago to Atlanta handcuffed to Al Capone while the latter was on his way to prison, arrived in Chicago yesterday. He had been taken from Atlanta to Jacksonville, Fla., where he was tried on a charge of transporting a stolen automobile across a state line. Convicted, he was given a prison term, but this was suspended and he was placed on probation. Morici promised that he was going straight in the future. He added that he had enjoyed the trip with the big gangster.

MAY 17, 1932

1932
Capone and a fellow prisoner (possibly Victor Morici), unrelated to Capone's case, on a train en route to Atlanta, Georgia.

PART III

MOB TARGETS

An early booking mug of Joe Aiello,
whose feud with Capone and
Antonio Lombardo was the source
of many mob hits in the 1920s.

JOE AIELLO HUNTED BY LAKE COUNTY AS MACHINE GUN RAIDER

Warrants for the arrest of Joseph Aiello, leader of a Sicilian clan of alcohol cookers, and Charles Connors, a lieutenant of the Bugs Moran gang, were forwarded to Chicago police headquarters from Waukegan yesterday by Col A. V. Smith, state's attorney of Lake county.

The two were charged with assault with deadly weapons in a complaint filed yesterday before Justice of the Peace, Harold J. Tallett at North Chicago, who issued the warrants. Col. Smith said he had information that Aiello and Connors were the machine gummers who removed thirteen slot machines from the Deep Lake resorts of Joseph Jackson and Henning Johnson on June 9.

Aiello and Connors were recognized as among the gangsters who have been holding target practice with machine guns at Mrs. Elizabeth Cassidy's resort at Bluff Lake. The place was raided Sunday but no gangsters were found.

Rumor has it that the Moran, Capone, and Druggan gangs are mobilizing for a struggle to control the beer and slot machine traffic among county resorts.

Prohibition agents yesterday broke up four stills and destroyed 4,500 gallons of mash housed in an old mansion at 1250 North State street and connect by an underground passage with a private garage in the rear. The place was operated by the Moran gang, according to the agents. Sam Vito, the still tender, was arrested.

JUNE 18, 1929

Seize Five in Assassination Plot

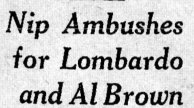

Nip Ambushes for Lombardo and Al Brown

Following the arrest of five men last night and the seizure of dynamite and firearms in rooms they occupied, Chief of Detectives William E. O'Connor announced a belief that the police had frustrated plans for the assassination of Tony Lombardo, Italian fraternal leader, and Al Brown, Cicero vice lord.

The leader of the five is Angelo La Mantio, who was seized in a room at the Rex hotel, 3142 North Ashland avenue. In his possession were found receipts showing that he had leased a flat at 4441 West Washington boulevard, across the street from the Lombardo home. When police raided the flat a few days ago two automatic shotguns were found hidden under the bed.

Admits Purchase of Guns.

There were other receipts in La Mantio's room, proving that he was the purchase of these guns and of several rifles and pistols. He readily admitted this, but declined to talk about what he proposed to do with the weapons.

NOVEMBER 21, 1927

NOVEMBER 1927

These men, all reputed enemies of Capone and Tony Lombardo, were held while Chicago police investigated a plot to kill members of a rival crime gang. From left are: Joseph Aiello, Joe Rubinelli, Michelo Bizirro, Jack Manzella, Joe Russo.

SEPTEMBER 11, 1928
Al Capone in the crowd at Antonio "The Scourge" Lombardo's funeral at Mount Carmel Cemetery in Hillside, Illinois. Lombardo, Capone's adviser, was gunned down six days earlier at the intersection of Madison and Dearborn Streets in Chicago.

The arrows, which appeared when the photo was originally published, are to possibly indicate men who are holding guns in their pockets.

GUNMEN BURY LOMBARDO WITH KINGLY POMP

Capone Holds Levee; Police Hunt Guns.

Lombardo, as a leader in the Italo-American National Union, the successor of the Unione Sicilione, with its membership of 15,000, was an important person. Al Capone, his partner, as the head of the extensive booze and vice and gambling syndicate, was another important person. Capone held court in the back yard. To get near him one had to pass the scrutiny and the questioning of several men who knew how to use their eyes. The funeral attendants were eager for the opportunity to shake Capone's hand. He was most gracious about it.

Gang gentlemen at funerals are usually a bit touchy about photographs. Other people might recognize the pictures and then there might be the annoyance of a trip to a cell for a brief period. But Capone said yesterday was a different occasion. They were burying a friend and an honored citizen.

Commissioner of Detectives Stego didn't speak of Lombardo as an honored citizen.

"Look over the hoodlums out there and you may see some of the fellows we want for many murders," he said. "Lombardo was a dangerous fellow and there'll be a lot of dangerous guys at his funeral."

SEPTEMBER 12, 1928

FEBRUARY 14, 1929
Onlookers watch police remove
bodies from the garage on North
Clark Street.

SLAY DOCTOR IN MASSACRE

OFFICIALS PROBE BOOZE DEALS IN GANG SHOOTING

Inquest Today in Seven Deaths.

In the state's attorney's investigation last night of the "north side massacre" in which seven men were shot dead against a wall in a garage at 2122 North Clark street yesterday morning a dovetailing of underworld rumors developed a double motive.

It is the police belief that the gangsters who were killed paid the penalty for being followers of George Moran, successor to Dean O'Banion. The historic antagonist, as history goes in the swift careers of gangsters, of the O'Banion-Moran crew, is Alphonse Capone, otherwise Al Brown.

See 20th Ward Motive.

While that historic antagonism furnished the police a background of hate, jealousy, and revenge, it was also reported that a more immediate reason for the seven murders lies in a campaign of Moran's alcohol sellers to take liquor from Detroit sources and with it penetrate the Bloody Twentieth ward, the booze territory of the Capone gang.

While the police under Commissioner Russell and State's Attorney Swanson were hunting evidence a special coroner's jury was impanelled by Coroner Bundesen to investigate the murders of the men listed and described as follows:

Dr. Reinhardt H. Schwimmer, resident of the Parkway hotel, an optometrist with offices in the Capitol building. Had no criminal record, but was known as the companion of hoodlums and was said to have boasted recently that he was in the alky racket and could have any one "taken for a ride."

Peter Gusenberg, 434 Roscoe street, for 27 years a criminal and one of the leaders of the Moran gang.

Albert R. Weinshank, owner of the Alcazar club, 4207 Broadway, and an official of the Central Cleaners and Dyers company. 2705 Fullerton avenue.

Adam Heyer, alias Frank Snyder, alias Haes, 2024 Farragut avenue, owner of the S. M. C. Cartage company, where the murders took place.

John May, 1249 West Madison street, father of seven children and ex-safe blower.

James Clark, brother-in-law of Bugs Moran, and said to have a reputation as a hardened killer.

Frank Gusenberg, brother of Peter, who died in the Alexian Brothers' hospital after refusing for an hour to give any information to the police about his assailants.

As officials viewed the bodies after the shooting they sought to locate Moran without success. But last night it was reported by friends of the gang chief that he was secluded and refused even to leave his room. Capone was found to be in Florida superintending his dog track venture there.

FEBRUARY 15, 1929

WHERE SEVEN MEMBERS OF MORAN GANG WERE LINED UP AGAINST WALL AND KILLED BY RIVALS. The garage at 2122 North Clark street, on the windows of which appear the name "S. M. C. Cartage company," in which massacre took place. Two of the executioners wore the uniforms and stars of city policemen.

GANG WIPED OUT. George (Bugs) Moran left a leader without followers.

MEMBERS AND ASSOCIATES OF MORAN GANG WHO WERE KILLED IN GARAGE. Left to right, upper row: Peter Gusenberg, former convict, and one of principal lieutenants of Moran; Frank Gusenberg, brother of Peter, who was left alive by assassins, but died of wounds; James Clark, brother-in-law of Moran. Lower row: Albert Weinshank, a recent recruit of the gang; Adam Heyer, who rented the garage in which he and his companions were slain; John May, auto mechanic, who is said by police to have been a former safe blower.

HOW THE VICTIMS OF THE GANGLAND MASSACRE FELL BEFORE FUSILLADE. Photodiagram showing how the bodies of the slain men lay in front of the north wall, against which they had been lined up before machine guns and shotgun were turned loose.

LOSES BROTHERS. Henry Gusenberg, whose two brothers were killed, leaving state's attorney's office.

RIVAL GANG CHIEF. Al Capone, foe of Moran, as he appears in Florida, where he is now.

OFFICIALS VISIT SCENE OF MASSACRE AND ANNOUNCE THEIR PLANS. Left to right: Police Commissioner William F. Russell, Coroner Herman N. Bundesen, and Lieut. William Cusack in the "S. M. C. Cartage company" garage.

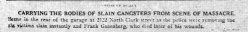

CARRYING THE BODIES OF SLAIN GANGSTERS FROM SCENE OF MASSACRE. Scene in the rear of the garage at 2122 North Clark street as the police were removing the six victims slain instantly and Frank Gusenberg, who died later of his wounds.

DOG HOWLS DISMALLY AFTER SEEING THE SLAUGHTER. Patrolman Zig Warchalowski holding animal that was badly frightened by assassins' fusillade.

TWO WOMEN WHO SAW THE ASSASSINS LEAVE GARAGE AFTER MASSACRE. At left: Mrs. Jeanette Landesman of 2124 North Clark street with her son, Robert; right: Mrs. Joe Morin, 2125 North Clark street, who said two slayers wore police uniforms.

Slay E. J. O'Hare, Race Track Head

ASSASSINS FIRE 2 BLASTS INTO FLEEING AUTO

Death Race Ends in Busy Ogden Avenue.

Edward J. O'Hare, wealthy president of Sportsman's park race track in Stickney, was shot to death in gangland fashion yesterday afternoon as he raced his automobile northeast in Ogden avenue, near Rockwell street, in a futile effort to outdistance his assassins. The killers drew up alongside, fired two shotgun charges into O'Hare's head and neck, then sped away.

The slaying presented a puzzle whose outer edges touched the gang kingdom of Al Capone, the world of horse and dog racing, and stretched 15 years into the past when O'Hare was convicted in connection with the collapse of the George Remus bootlegging syndicate.

TRIPLE INQUIRY STARTED.

Police and state's attorney's investigators last night were pressing three inquiries, one of which they believe may solve the slaying. They said there are three major possibilities:

1. That O'Hare quarreled with certain associates over the proceeds of the prosperous racing meet at Sportsman's Park, which closed last Saturday. The dispute, they believe, may have reached an impasse shortly before the slaying, the killers trailing O'Hare from the track's offices at 33d street and Laramie avenue.

2. That the underworld suspected him of having given information to the federal government. A memorandum found on the body indicated a close association between O'Hare and the federal bureau of investigation.

3. That the slaying and the imminent release from prison of Al Capone might be connected. It was recalled that Cicero and Stickney, where O'Hare's interested have expanded so rapidly since 1932, are Capone's old stronghold.

NOVEMBER 9, 1939

O'Hare Warned of Capone's Rage

TELL HOW GANG CZAR RESENTED RISE TO POWER

Slain Track Chief's Hideout Found.

Mystery! Where's Al?

Washington, D.C. Nov. 12 (Special)—The whereabouts of Al Capone became a mystery tonight after reports were circulated that he had been release from the federal prison on Terminal Island, Cal. It was reported that Capone had been taken out of the prison and was headed for a hospital for further treatment for paresis. His release was scheduled to take place next Sunday.

For more than two years before his shotgun assassination last Wednesday Eddie J. O'Hare, millionaire front man for the Capone gang syndicate, lived in the knowledge that two convicts freed from Alcatraz said that Al Capone was angry "at Eddie" and was making threats against him.

This was learned yesterday. Investigators who have been seeking the shotgun murderers have been convinced from the start that O'Hare's death must have been decreed by the gang. They reasoned that no other mob would have dared to harm the Capone organization's front man without at least its acquiescence.

O'Hare, it is now learned, received this warning from a friend of the two convicts. Whether or not they knew O'Hare is not clear, but their friend did. The released convicts told this friend of O'Hare that Capone was raging against his race track manager. Investigators could only speculate on what aroused Capone's wrath.

NOVEMBER 13, 1939

An undated photo of the nattily dressed Edward Spike O'Donnell, who survived more than a dozen assassination attempts, was an outspoken Capone rival and beer runner during Prohibition. "Life with me is just one bullet after another," he once said. O'Donnell died in 1962 of a heart at age 72.

O'Donnell, Beer Baron of 20s, Dies

Edward J. [Spike] O'Donnell, 72, who defied more than a dozen attempts to assassinate him during his career as one of Chicago's prohibition era beer barons, died of a heart attack last night in his home at 8234 Loomis av....

The natural death of O'Donnell closed the book on one of the most violent and flamboyant figures who dominated the roaring 1920s in Chicago....

O'Donnell emerged triumphant in a struggle with Joe Saltis for the control of beer running on Chicago's southwest side. He then engaged in a battle with syndicate chief Johnny Torrio and his lieutenant, Al Capone, for city-wide control of beer distribution.

AUGUST 27, 1962

PART IV

CAPONE'S DEATH

Al Capone Dies in Florida Villa

Heart Fails After Stroke of Apoplexy

Miami Beach, Jan 25 (/P)—Scarface Al Capone, Chicago prohibition era mobster, died in his villa here at 6:25 [Chicago time] tonight. He was 48.

"Death came very suddenly," said Dr. Kenneth S. Phillips, who has been attending the ex-gang leader since he was stricken with apoplexy last Tuesday.

Alphonse Capone personified an era. For the greater part of a decade he was Chicago's most publicized criminal: the figurehead universally chosen to illustrate the breakdown of law and order that followed the effort to legislate alcoholic beverages out of America.

JANUARY 26, 1947

The Capone era ended not in gunfire, but from a heart attack in his South Florida home on January 25, 1947. Here, a photographer snaps what he or she believes to be Al Capone's casket arriving in Chicago; however, it was later revealed that Capone's casket had been driven from Florida by hearse (see article on page 133).

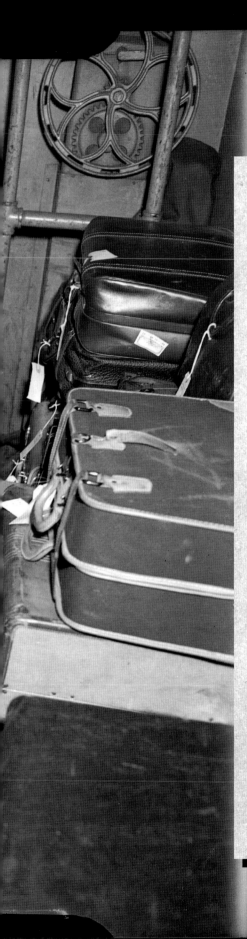

CAPONE'S BODY ARRIVES HERE FOR INTERMENT

Capone's body was brought home yesterday after a two day trip by hearse from Miami. The black vehicle crept slowly over icy roads to the south gate of the cemetery as a black sedan, believed to be carrying members of Capone's family, followed.

The homecoming was a far cry from the days of the gangster's power, and the hearse trip from Florida was made in typical gangland secrecy.

Other Kin Arrive on Train

No lavish display awaited him. His body went to a receiving vault where it will lie until city authorities grant formal permission for the interment.

A shipping permit from Florida authorities accompanied the hearse and was left with cemetery authorities. A Chicago undertaking firm made arrangements for the hush-hush trip.

Other members of Capone's family, who had been expected to accompany his body, were aboard an Illinois Central train which arrived in the city at 8:15 last night.

The family was reported to have traveled in a private Pullman car, which was transferred to the Illinois Central train from a Florida road at Birmingham, Ala., at 2:30 a.m. yesterday. Until Capone's body arrived via hearse it was believed it was in the baggage car of the same train.

FEBRUARY 2, 1947

FEBRUARY 1, 1947
Another photo of what was believed to be Al Capone's casket, taken at Illinois Central Station. Central Station was a terminal in downtown Chicago, located at Roosevelt Road and Michigan Avenue, on the southern end of Grant Park.

CAPONE'S BODY ARRIVES TODAY; BARE BIG DEBT

The body of Al Capone, Chicago's prohibition gang czar, will be brought here today for burial, according to information from Miami. The body left there Thursday morning and, it is believed, will be brought here by hearse for burial in Mount Olivet cemetery. It was not learned whether a wake would be held first in Rago Brothers funeral home at 624 N. Western av.

Capone died of pneumonia after a stroke of apoplexy in his palatial home on Palm Island, Miami Beach, last Saturday. He was 48.

The former gangster died without any property in his name. His 25 room Palm Island home was mortgaged for $35,000 by his wife, Mae, in 1936 while Capone was serving in Alcatraz penitentiary for income tax evasion. The mortgage is now held by Frank Harmon, loop night club owner.

FEBRUARY 1, 1947

GRAVE RECEIVES ORCHID-DECKED CAPONE CASKET

Brief Service Held at Mount Olivet

Al Capone was buried yesterday in a simple ceremony in Mount Olivet cemetery. The brief committal rite was performed by Msgr. William J. Gorman while relatives, friends, and curious gathered in the near zero cold about the grave of the prohibition era gangster.

A blanket of gardenias, topped with a few orchids, was spread over the heavy bronze casket after it was removed from the cemetery vault where it was placed last Saturday after being brought here by hearse from Miami Beach.

The only pallbearers were grave diggers who carried the casket from a hearse into the shelter tent erected over the grave. The hearse was used to transport the body from the cemetery vault to the grave area.

In contrast to prohibition era gang funerals at which dozens of policemen mingled in the crowds, only two were assigned to Capone's burial. They were Lt. James B. Folsom and Sgt. Raymond McGrath of the Bedford Park county highway police station....

When the service was finished, the mourners were helped back to the cars and the procession moved away. Over the casket, workmen lowered the vault's heavy bronze top, engraved, "Rest In Peace."

FEBRUARY 5, 1947

Al Capone's grave is dug at Mount Olivet cemetery.

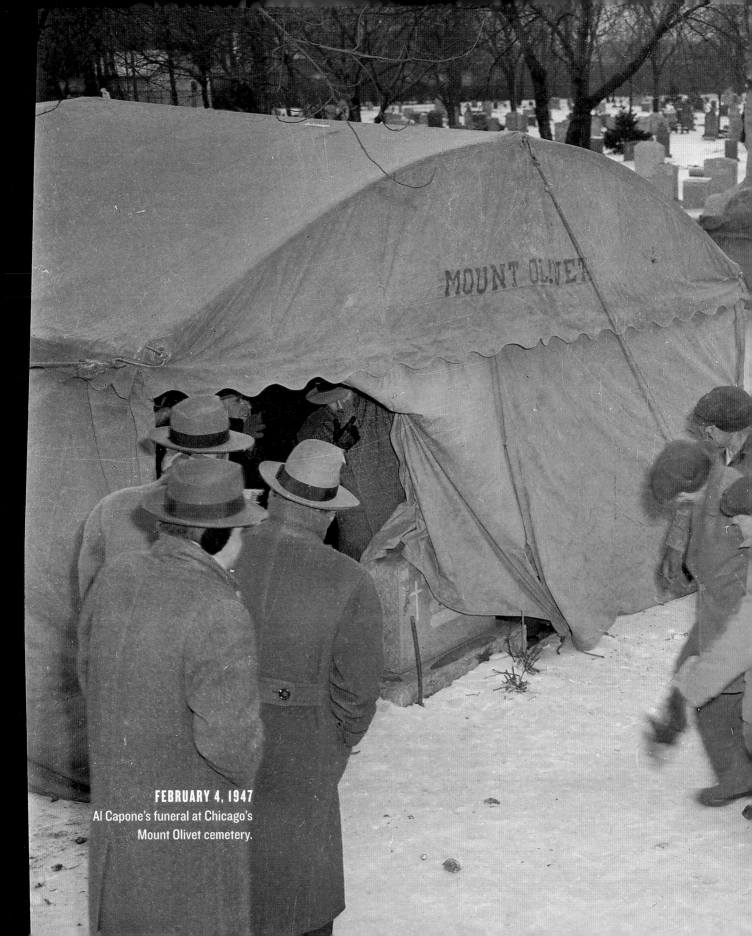

FEBRUARY 4, 1947
Al Capone's funeral at Chicago's
Mount Olivet cemetery.

ARTICLE CREDITS

Page 4   "STRIKE DOWN GANG RULE." *Chicago Daily Tribune* (1923-1963), October 5, 1926.

6   "RAID 3 CAPONE HIDEAWAYS, BUT MISS GANG CHIEF: Raids in Berwyn Show Guards on Duty." *Chicago Daily Tribune* (1923-1963), December 1, 1930.

10   "MIAMI DESTINED TO BE RULED BY KING SCARFACE: Capone Making Things Hum at Winter Resort." *Chicago Daily Tribune* (1923-1963), February 28, 1929.

9   "YOU CAN ALL GO THIRSTY…" *Chicago Daily Tribune* (1923-1963), December 6, 1927.

14   "RALPH CAPONE'S IN AGAIN, IF THAT MEANS ANYTHING: Gangster Faces New Gun Charge, but—." *Chicago Daily Tribune* (1923-1963), October 7, 1928.

17-18   Wood, Percy. "Prepare Feast for Capone's Return: GANG LEADER'S KIN EXPECT HIM BACK…" *Chicago Daily Tribune* (1923-1963), March 16, 1930.

21   "SISTER OF CAPONE, HIS CHIEF DEFENDER, EAGERLY AWAITS HIM." *Chicago Daily Tribune* (1923-1963), March 17, 1930.

25   "HITS WOMAN IN COURT." *Chicago Daily Tribune* (1923-1963), September 19, 1930.

27   "HUSH, HUSH." *Chicago Daily Tribune* (1923-1963), September 14, 1931.

36   "Ralph Capone and 9 Seized for Beer Quiz: RAIDERS ARREST RALPH CAPONE…" *Chicago Daily Tribune* (1923-1963), August 23, 1934.

39-40   "Kefauver to Give City Full Testimony of Police Captains: O'Connor to…" *Chicago Daily Tribune* (1923-1963), December 21, 1950.

41   "LASHES CAPONE, VOIDS CHARGE OF TAX EVASION: Court Decides Note Protected Hoodlum." *Chicago Daily Tribune* (1923-1963), November 22, 1952.

45   "TORRIO IS SHOT; POLICE HUNT FOR O'BANION MEN: Rum Czar's Driver Is Also Hit." *Chicago Daily Tribune* (1923-1963), Janunary 25, 1925.

49   "CAPONE, 4 AIDS FINED $2,601 IN JOLIET COURTS: Plead Guilty on Charges of Carrying Guns." *Chicago Daily Tribune* (1923-1963), December 23, 1927.

51   "CAPONE TO FACE U. S. JURY, BUT HE FEARS CITY COPS: Also He Wants Immunity on…" *Chicago Daily Tribune* (1923-1963), March 19, 1929.

51   "CAPONE, AS U. S. WITNESS, SHUNS HIS OLD HAUNTS: Crowd Jams Streets to See Gang Chief." *Chicago Daily Tribune* (1923-1963), March 21, 1929.

53   "U.S. CITES CAPONE FOR CONTEMPT; DOUBTS 'ILLNESS': Warrant Served After 2d Grand…" *Chicago Daily Tribune* (1923-1963), March 28, 1929.

54   "U. S. SUMMONS AL CAPONE TO COURT MONDAY: Gang Leader Must Face Contempt Charge." *Chicago Daily Tribune* (1923-1963), December 13, 1930.

60, 62   "'SICK' CAPONE'S JAUNTS TOLD: U. S. WITNESSES SAY GANG CHIEF ATTENDED…" *Chicago Daily Tribune* (1923-1963), February 26, 1931.

63   "CAPONE TO JAIL." *Chicago Daily Tribune* (1923-1963), March 2, 1931.

64   "CAPONE OBJECTS TO 'SCARFACE' IN WARRANT; WINS: Vagrancy Trial Is Set for March." *Chicago Daily Tribune* (1923-1963), March 5, 1931.

76   "CAPONE VAGRANT CASE DROPPED; LACK EVIDENCE." *Chicago Daily Tribune* (1923-1963), April 4, 1931.

PHOTO CREDITS

All photos from the *Chicago Tribune* historical archives.

81   "CAPONE BREWERY RUNNING ONLY 5 DAYS
      IS RAIDED: Destroy Plant and Beer Worth…"
      Chicago Daily Tribune (1923-1963), April 12, 1931.

82   "Capone Indicted by U. S.; Surrenders: GANGSTER
      GIVES $50,000 BOND IN…" *Chicago Daily
      Tribune* (1923-1963), June 6, 1931.

85   "Al Capone in Hands of Judge Today: CHIEF OF
      GANGS WAITS DECISION ON…" *Chicago Daily
      Tribune* (1923-1963), July 30, 1931.

87   "CAPONE 'DEAL' RULING TODAY: JUDGE
      REFUSES TO BE BOUND TO EASY…" *Chicago
      Daily Tribune* (1923-1963), July 31, 1931.

89   "CALL CAPONE JURORS TODAY:…" *Chicago
      Daily Tribune* (1923-1963), October 5, 1931.

92-93 Kinsley, Philip. "U.S. to Begin Its Capone Evidence
      Today: JURY IS CHOSEN IN OPENING…"
      Chicago Daily Tribune (1923-1963), October 7,
      1931.

96   Kinsley, Philip. "CAPONE'S TRAIL OF GOLD
      TRACED IN LUXURY SALES: $12,500 for
      an Auto…" *Chicago Daily Tribune* (1923-1963),
      October 13, 1931.

102   "U. S. May Place Al Capone in Cell Pending His
      Appeal." *Chicago Daily Tribune* (1923-1963),
      October 20, 1931.

105   "CAPONE SENTENCED." *Chicago Daily Tribune*
      (1923-1963), October 26, 1931.

107   Manly, Chesly. "CHICAGO PUBLIC ENEMY NO. 1
      NOW CONVICT 40886: Gates at Atlanta Close…"
      Chicago Daily Tribune (1923-1963), May 5, 1932.

109   "Capone's Companion on Prison Trip Back Home."
      Chicago Daily Tribune (1923-1963), May 17, 1932.

113   "JOE AIELLO HUNTED BY LAKE COUNTY AS
      MACHINE GUN RAIDER." *Chicago Daily
      Tribune* (1923-1963), June 18, 1929.

115   "Seize Five in Assassination Plot: Nip Ambushes for
      Lombardo and Al…" *Chicago Daily Tribune* (1923-
      1963), November 21, 1927.

117   "GUNMEN BURY LOMBARDO WITH KINGLY
      POMP: Capone Holds Levee; Police…" *Chicago
      Daily Tribune* (1923-1963), September 12, 1928.

120-121 "SLAY DOCTOR IN MASSACRE:
      OFFICIALS PROBE BOOZE DEALS IN GANG
      SHOOTING…" *Chicago Daily Tribune* (1923-
      1963), February 15, 1929.

123   "Slay E. J. O'Hare, Race Track Head: ASSASSINS
      FIRE 2 BLASTS INTO…" *Chicago Daily Tribune*
      (1923-1963), November 9, 1939.

125   "O'Hare Warned of Capone's Rage: TELL HOW
      GANG CZAR RESENTED RISE TO…" *Chicago
      Daily Tribune* (1923-1963), November 13, 1939.

127   "O'Donnell, Beer Baron of 20s, Dies: THE 20s
      BARON OF BEER SPIKE…" *Chicago Daily
      Tribune* (1923-1963), August 27, 1962.

131   "Al Capone Dies in Florida Villa: Heart Fails After
      Stroke of Apoplexy…" *Chicago Daily Tribune*
      (1923-1963), January 26, 1947.

133   "CAPONE'S BODY ARRIVES TODAY; BARE
      BIG DEBT." *Chicago Daily Tribune* (1923-1963),
      February 1, 1947.

133   "CAPONE'S BODY ARRIVES HERE FOR
      INTERMENT." *Chicago Daily Tribune* (1923-1963),
      February 2, 1947.

134   "Capone's Son at Burial: GRAVE RECEIVES
      ORCHID-DECKED CAPONE CASKET…"
      Chicago Daily Tribune (1923-1963), February 5,
      1947.